The Four Gospels

The Four Gospels

By

DOM JOHN CHAPMAN

1944

SHEED & WARD

New York

Copyright, 1944, by Sheed & Ward, Inc.

NIHIL OBSTAT
    RICARDUS DAVEY
        CENSOR DEPUTATUS, DIE 20 JULII 1943

IMPRIMATUR
    ✠ HERBERTUS BYRNE
        ABBAS PRAESES, DIE 21 JULII 1943

Second Printing, June, 1944

MANUFACTURED IN THE UNITED STATES OF AMERICA
BY BURR PRINTING HOUSE, INC., NEW YORK

Foreword

IN NOVEMBER 1927 Dom John Chapman, then Prior of Downside, was invited to give four conferences to the Catholic undergraduates at Cambridge. He chose as his subject "The Four Gospels." These conferences were so full of interest that it seemed to the present writer and to many others who were privileged to hear them, that they should be published. After Abbot Chapman's death in 1933, the manuscript was discovered among his papers, and the careful revision of which it showed traces indicated that the author may himself have contemplated publication. But it was considered wiser to delay the publication of the conferences until the Abbot's more fully detailed and documented study of the Synoptic Problem could be issued. In 1937 this condition was fulfilled by the appearance of his masterly volume *Matthew, Mark and Luke*, posthumously edited by Mgr. John M. T. Barton.

In preparing these conferences for publication, only minor alterations have been found necessary. They are printed almost exactly as they were first written and delivered. The Introduction (here given as a separate section) was originally combined with the conference on St. Matthew's Gospel.

An Appendix has been added in which are set out (1) the chief Patristic texts bearing on the authorship, date of composition, and mutual relationship of the Gospels, and (2) the Replies of the Pontifical Biblical Commission on these and similar questions. An examination of these documents will show how completely Abbot Chapman's views are in accord with ancient tradition and the mind of the Church.

A. G. M.

Contents

Introduction

THE CHRISTIAN WRITERS of the end of the second century accepted the Gospels just as we do. So obvious was it, and so certain were they that there were four and only four, that they used curious mystical and allegorical comparisons. St. Irenaeus, writing little more than eighty years after the last Gospel was published, declared that there must be four Gospels, because there are four regions of the world to be evangelised and four winds to carry the Gospel everywhere, since the Church is to spread throughout the world; the four Gospels are the four Cherubim of Ezechiel, carrying the revelation of God to man, the four living creatures of St. John's Apocalypse—man, lion, ox, eagle. St. Irenaeus knows of no doubt within the Church as to these four Gospels. He writes as an elderly man, born and educated in the province of Asia, probably at Smyrna, and afterwards priest and then bishop at Lyons in Gaul; so he is witness for East and West. In his early manhood he had known St. Polycarp, the martyr-bishop of Smyrna, and remembered well, he tells us, the stories Polycarp used to relate of his master St. John the Apostle, who had published his Gospel while dwelling at Ephesus, and had died there as late as the reign of Trajan—that is, after January 98.

We can go back behind St. Irenaeus. St. Justin the philosopher, who lived near Jerusalem, was martyred at Rome about 165. In his writings he quotes all the four Gospels, and his disciple Tatian combined them into a *Diatessaron* or life of Christ in the words of the four evangelists. St. Justin's witness carries us far back, for he represents his *Dialogue with the Jew Trypho* as a conversation between himself and this Jew about the year 133 at Ephesus—that is, about thirty-five years after the Apostle John's death in that city.

Again, the Gnostic heresies of the Egyptian Valentinus and his followers arose between 120 and 130. They used all our four Gospels, evidently finding them universally acknowledged. One of them, Heracleon, wrote a commentary on St. John's Gospel during the reign of Hadrian, that is, before 138, and therefore less than forty years after the Gospel was written. Without referring to any other evidence, the witnesses I have mentioned suffice to show us that our four Gospels were accepted in the first quarter of the second century. Tradition, acceptance, implies many previous years of habitual use, and carries us back at the lowest computation to the historical date of the fourth Gospel —about 97-98.

Now the Gospel of St. John attests the other three Gospels. It can be shown to quote them all three, when it occasionally touches the same events. It is written to supplement them, and presupposes a knowledge of them, and would have been unintelligible without them. It omits many of the most important events in Our Lord's life but supposes them known. The statements of ancient Fathers that St. John added his Gospel to the other three and approved them is thus amply confirmed by the evidence of the Gospel itself.

Another line of evidence has an interest of its own —the history of the text.

The earliest manuscripts of the original Greek or of the most ancient versions, the Old Syriac and Old Latin, only carry us back to the fourth and fifth centuries, the fragments of papyri of earlier date being infinitesimally small. But quotations by the earliest Fathers bring us back much further. These manuscripts and versions and quotations establish *three* main types of text. The first family called the κοινή or common Byzantine text, also called *textus receptus,* or Lucianic, cannot be certainly traced before the end of the third century. The second, rather oddly called "the Western text," lies behind the earliest Syriac and Latin translations. It is the worst text, being full of harmonistic alterations of words, to make one Gospel agree with another. It is famous for its numerous interpolations, many (it seems) from Apostolic tradition. This very corrupt "Western" text is the earliest attested. It was used in the second century by St. Justin, St. Irenaeus, Clement of Alexandria,

Tertullian and others. It cannot have arisen much later than the year 100, and testifies to the coexistence of the four Gospels, the Acts and St. Paul's Epistles, by the harmonistic alterations which make them alike, and by the similarity in character of the additions and corruptions of the text. The astonishing fact, unquestioned among textual critics, that the text used by learned Christians in the second century, was a corrupt text full of careful emendations and improvements, is a curious and ineluctible demonstration that the genuine text itself was older.

The third family of text is far the best, though not to be followed without caution; it was called by Westcott and Hort the "neutral" text and by von Soden (without sufficient reason) the "Hesychian." It is found in the two ancient Greek Bibles of the fourth century —the *Codex Sinaiticus,* discovered in 1844 by Tischendorf in a waste-paper basket in the monastery of St. Catherine on Mount Sinai, and the yet more famous *Codex Vaticanus,* the most venerable book in the world.

The manuscripts and the versions are unanimous like the Fathers in giving to the Gospels the titles they now have. There are naturally a few variations in the order, due to copyists. The Old Latin translation, before St. Jerome's revision, set the Apostles first, thus: Matthew, John, Luke, Mark. But the present order, Matthew, Mark, Luke, John, was already traditional in the days of St. Irenaeus. It was regarded as a chronological order by all the ancients. (I do not admit Clement of Alexandria to be an exception.*) An infinitesimally small number of exceptions put St. John first. Otherwise Matthew is always the first Gospel in the manuscripts, the versions and the Fathers.

The authenticity of the four Gospels has enormously more testimony than can be collected for most of the Greek and Latin classics. It is especially impressive to note that the muddle-headed arguments of "liberals" against their genuineness have never moved anyone, as a rule, who did not already wish to doubt it because he already disbelieved or doubted the Incarnation. I know it is frequently urged (by journalists or novelists, for example) that German critics have so successfully assailed the Gospels, that no reasonable person has any right to doubt their late and composite character. But the fact remains that the critics have never succeeded in evolving any theory which won consent. No one believes in their hypotheses except because he is induced to do so by his theological position.

* Clement gives priority to Matthew and Luke because they alone give genealogies of Christ. See Appendix, p. 68. ED.

The Gospel of St. Matthew

THE FIRST GOSPEL in rank is St. Matthew. We have early witness that it was regarded as the first to be written, and there is absolutely no ancient witness to the contrary. It is taken by the earliest harmonists, Tatian in the second century, Ammonius in the third, Eusebius in the fourth, as giving the framework of the life of Christ to which they attach what the other Gospels add. The title of the Gospel has always been κατὰ Ματθαῖον or εὐαγγέλιον κατὰ Ματθαῖον. The textual witness to this as its original title is quite conclusive, nor does antiquity supply us with any suggestion that the Gospel was not written by the Apostle St. Matthew. From the time we have any Christian writings, we find St. Matthew quoted more than any other Gospel. In the days of the Fathers and up to the present day, more commentaries have been written on St. Matthew than on any other Gospel. It is not only the first book of the New Testament, but it is from many points of view the most important.

It is also on the whole the best Greek in the New Testament, together with the Epistle to the Hebrews and the Epistle of St. James. These three books are the only three of which ancient tradition says they are not originals, but translations from the Aramaic. They are also the only three books of the New Testament which were certainly addressed to Jewish converts and not to Gentiles.

With regard to St. Matthew the evidence of antiquity is unanimous and extraordinarily early, that he wrote for the Jews of Palestine in Hebrew, that is, Aramaic—"in their dialect," as St. Irenaeus puts it. Papias, Irenaeus, Origen, Eusebius, Jerome, are our most famous authorities for this. St. Papias, whose life was divided between the first century and the second, who had known St. John and the daughters of St. Philip, and had collected the traditions of the elders who had lived with the Apostles, tells us on the authority of one of the ancients: "Matthew composed his Gospel (τὰ λογία) in Hebrew, and everyone translated it as he could." This assumes the subsequent existence of the universally received Greek translation which we now use. "Liberal" critics have done their best to explain away this testimony by mistranslation of λογία to mean "discourses" and by then wildly referring the words to some lost collection of discourses of Matthew!

For the Protestants from the sixteenth century onwards, because they taught the verbal inspiration of Scripture, declared the Greek St. Matthew to be an original not a translation, and this has been an almost universal dogma among Protestants up to the present day. At this moment most Protestant critics make the same assertion with a more scientific reason; they think St. Matthew is founded on St. Mark, in which case it was necessarily written in Greek, and these Protestant critics contradict all the historical evidence with a light heart.

Ancient writers pointed out that whereas the lists of the Apostles in Matthew, Mark, Luke and Acts all mention St. Matthew's name, only St. Matthew's own Gospel adds the words "the publican," for to be a tax-gatherer or "publican" was regarded by the Jews as the worst disgrace. So he relates his own call by Christ, when sitting at the seat of custom, whereas St. Mark and St. Luke, telling the same story, give the name Levi instead of Matthew so as to shield St. Matthew from the infamy of his former calling.

Even a cursory comparison of the first Gospel with the others, shows that it was intended for Jews—not proselytes, nor Hellenists, but Jews of Palestine. It begins with a genealogy tracing Our Lord from the tribe of Judah and from King David and through all the kings of Judah, and showing him to be born of a virgin to fulfil the prophecy of Isaiah. He is born in Bethlehem, the city of David, and adored as King of the Jews by wise men of the Gentiles. He is prophesied by John the Baptist and baptized by him. He prepares for his public ministry by a forty days' fast, and rejects the temptation by the Devil to make himself King over all the world.

Then he begins to preach "the Kingdom of Heaven," more accurately "the Reign of the Heavens." This was a common expression of the Rabbis and was familiar to the Jews to whom Our Lord preached. The word "Heaven" was used for "God," just as instead of "Jehovah" the Jews read "the Lord" and in conversation said "the Name." Thus "the Kingdom (which is old English for 'Reign') of God" in the other Gospels and Acts and St. Paul, is exactly the same as "the Kingdom of Heaven" in St. Matthew. But a Greek Christian, or even a Greek proselyte among the Jews, might easily mistake the meaning of "the Kingdom of Heaven" and suppose it to mean "the next world." It is obvious that St. Matthew, who alone says "Kingdom of Heaven," was writing for Jews, and that in the Greek St. Matthew we have a translation of the ordinary Aramaic expression. It is difficult to conceive that so ambiguous an expression as "Kingdom of Heaven" was used in a Gospel written in Greek. It seems to be one of the clear indications that this Gospel is really a translation. St. Matthew also uses a beautiful periphrasis to avoid using the word "God," twenty times writing "your Father in Heaven" or "your Heavenly Father." This was an expression much used by the Jews and would come naturally in an Aramaic Gospel; though St. Matthew, being a

Christian, does not invariably avoid the word "God."

St. Matthew shows Jesus to be the Christ, the Messiah, or anointed, the King who brings in the Reign of God. He exhibits Our Lord as teaching with absolute authority a New Law which raises the Old Law of Moses by completing it. He gives a series of contrasts: "You have heard that it was said by them of old time . . . but I say to you . . ." He makes plain Our Lord's view of the teachers of his time, the traditions of the Rabbis, the hypocritical exaggerations concerning the Sabbath, the sham piety of the Pharisees, and the worldliness and materialism of the Sadducees. Christ refutes their arguments and vanquishes them. They are furious, and bring him before the Roman Governor. He is put to death, and rises again, and sends out his disciples to convert the world, saying: "All power is given to me in Heaven and on earth."

If we compare all this with the other evangelists, we shall find that most of the matter peculiar to Matthew is concerned with the Jews or the fulfilment of prophecy. All the Gospels teach that Jesus is the Messiah, the Saviour of the world, and the Son of God; but St. John especially shows him as Son of God, St. Luke as Saviour, and St. Matthew above all as the Messiah, whom the Jews in their wickedness rejected, but had even yet the chance of accepting.

Thus the old Protestant view, still current, that St. Matthew wrote in Greek, appears as a paradox, for his Gospel was meant for the Aramaic-speaking Jews of Palestine. Still more paradoxical is the view that it was based on St. Mark and is later than St. Luke. We should have to believe that the Gospels for the Gentiles were first written, and then adapted in 70 or 80 by many additions and excisions, and furnished with prophecies from the Old Testament, for the use of those Jews of Palestine who had already been massacred or dispersed in the Jewish War of Vespasian and Titus! First the Gentile then the Jew, is evidently a topsy-turvy theory.

As we read St. Matthew today, the chief characteristic which strikes us is not the frequent reference to prophecy, nor the reference to the Old Law, but the incomparable sermons of Our Lord which it contains. There is less incident in St. Matthew than in the other Gospels. Many miracles are told, but tersely and briefly; and the great spaces are filled with the public teaching of Christ.

First of all comes the greatest of all sermons, the Sermon on the Mount, which fills all chapters 5, 6 and 7, full of astonishing doctrine from the very first words "Blessed are the poor" onwards. It is too familiar to us to be striking, unless we take the trouble to read it as if we had never heard it before; and then its pregnant sentences become as telling and trenchant and wonderful as they are convincing. From a purely literary point of view, the development and logical division are admirable, and the rhythmical repetitions give a peculiarity of form which is as much poetical as oratorical. Some portions, especially towards the end, are less developed and read like summaries, as though the short-hand writer were growing tired. (St. Luke has a very much shorter account of this sermon, though he takes up some of the omitted bits in other connexions.)

The next great discourse (ch. 10) is to the Apostles when they are sent out to preach, only the commencement being in St. Mark and St. Luke. The eleventh chapter has a discourse most of which is in St. Luke also, and the same is true of chapter 12. The thirteenth chapter consists of a series of parables about the Kingdom of Heaven, of which only half are given by Mark and Luke. The "woes" against the Pharisees and scribes (ch. 23) are in a much shorter form in St. Luke. A very long discourse on the destruction of Jerusalem and the end of the world takes up chapters 24 and 25. Much less than half is reproduced by St. Mark followed by St. Luke, and the latter has a few other verses of it elsewhere. But the great parables which conclude it (in chapter 25) are in St. Matthew only: the parable of the Talents, the Ten Virgins, and the great symbolic account of the Last Judgement.

Renan said of St. Luke's Gospel that it is "le plus

beau livre qui ait jamais été écrit." But St. Luke gives
mainly that part of Our Lord's teaching which was
useful for Gentile converts, and puts it together in
short pieces with but little connexion, interspersed
with a great number of incidents. St. Mark gives very
little of Our Lord's teaching. St. John is full of sub-
lime teaching, largely in the form of conversations or
even arguments. But it is St. Matthew who gives us
the completest idea of Our Lord's life and teaching
in Galilee and Jerusalem as it appeared to his hearers,
Galilaeans and Jews. The others supplement Matthew, and St. Luke reproduces a large part of the same
teaching, just as St. Mark recounts the same incidents.

Matthew is the most perfect in literary form, in
logical sequence, in definite arrangement. Each incident is perfectly told, and each discourse is an oratorical development and an admirable whole. The entire
Gospel is a carefully coordinated unity. It gives a
complete framework for the details added by the
others.

So much of it is found again in Mark and Luke,
that it is well to remember, not only how admirably
set all these borrowed passages appear in St. Matthew,
how logically they hang together and how harmoni-
ously they combine, but also how beautiful is the
rhythm of the discourses with their antistrophic repetitions, and lastly, how many wonderful passages are
found in St. Matthew only.

Let me end by recalling some of the incomparable sayings in St. Matthew alone:

"Blessed are the meek, for they shall possess the earth" (v. 4)

"Blessed are the clean of heart, for they shall see God" (v. 8)

or the little parables; such as:

"The Kingdom of heaven is like to a merchant seeking good pearls, who when he had found one pearl of great price, went his way, and sold all that he had and bought it" (xiii. 45-46)

or again:

"Come to me, all you that labour and are burdened, and I will refresh you. Take my yoke upon you and learn of me, for I am meek and humble of heart, and you shall find rest to your souls. For my yoke is sweet and my burden light" (xi. 28-30).

The Gospel of St. Mark

THE MOST REMARKABLE literary point about the Gospels is that three of them cover nearly the same ground; for Matthew, Mark and Luke have the greater part of their framework of incidents in common. Hence they are called the three "Synoptists" of the "Synoptic Gospels," as distinguished from St. John. The fourth Gospel is evidently a supplement, and, except in giving the story of Our Lord's Passion, it repeats only two or three incidents which were given in the other Gospels.

Nearly all the matter of St. Mark's Gospel is found also in St. Matthew, and two thirds of it are found also in St. Luke. In fact, all three Synoptic Gospels agree as to about two thirds of St. Mark, or nearly half of St. Luke, or rather less than half of St. Matthew (who describes incidents in fewer words). The matter which is common to all three Synoptists is sometimes called "the triple tradition."

If the whole of this "triple tradition" is written out or printed side by side in parallel columns in Greek, and the words which agree in all three Gospels or any two are underlined, certain things are at once evident:

In the first place, all three agree in a great number of Greek words, in unusual expressions, even in curious constructions. Either they have copied each other, or all have copied some common source in Greek.

In the second place, Mark often agrees in wording with Matthew against Luke, and often with Luke against Matthew, but Matthew and Luke practically never agree in wording against Mark (except in a few cases where Luke, who always keeps St. Mark's order, has some fragment out of order, agreeing with Matthew rather than Mark). Hence Mark is regularly a mean between Matthew and Luke, whose likeness to each other is only caused by their agreement with Mark. A common source for all three will not explain why Mark is the mean between Matthew and Luke. This is not only true of a lost *written* source, used by all three evangelists, but also of a common *oral* source, which was a few years ago a popular hypothesis. It was imagined that the early Christians were made to learn the life of Christ by heart, and that in this way it was handed down by word of mouth; it was thought that the likeness of wording between the three Synoptic Gospels was thus accounted for, as well as their curious differences. But this hypothesis did not account for the agreement of Matthew and Luke with Mark but not with each other. Besides, there is no probability that the Christians of the first century learned the life of Christ by heart any more than the Christians of other centuries. The catechetical instruction of the Church is represented in substance by the modern Catechism and not by the Gospels. The Creed was always learnt by heart. The Orientals, no doubt, had much oral teaching, and used their memories to a considerable extent. But that Gentile Christians ever did so is vastly improbable, and no trace of such a custom exists. Anyhow such a Gospel learnt by heart must have first been written down. This hypothesis is little to the fore now-a-days, as it raises difficulties and really explains none.

As Mark is the mean between Matthew and Luke, only three schemes of literary dependence are possible.

Suppose the order: Luke, Mark, Matthew—Luke used by Mark and Mark by Matthew. But no one holds that Luke wrote first, and nearly all critics, Catholic and non-Catholic, are by this time convinced that St. Luke used the Gospel of St. Mark, just as we now have it, as his principal authority. Hence two possibilities remain: either Matthew used Mark, or Mark used Matthew. Both these suppositions are so far satisfactory. If Matthew used Mark and Luke used Mark, then the likeness in the "triple tradition" between Matthew and Luke will only be in words which they have borrowed from Mark, and this is the case. This view is the dominant one at the present time among non-Catholic critics. They regard St. Mark as the first of the Gospels to be written, and they confirm this by his freshness and liveliness which show that we have the words of an eye-witness. Matthew and Luke are then said to have independently completed Mark, who gave no account of Our Lord's Birth and very little of his teaching. So Matthew and Luke added from totally different sources their story of the Nativity and Childhood, and a great amount of discourses and parables, more than half being from a very early collection of discourses even older than Mark, called "Q," the initial of the word "Quelle," German for "source."

Of this imaginary document "Q," I have nothing to say here.* But as to Mark's being the first Gospel, it is necessary to point out that this contradicts all the ancient evidence, since the tradition throughout the second century assures us without hesitation that St. Matthew's was the first Gospel. Secondly, the same ancient tradition, almost contemporary, assures us that St. Matthew wrote in Hebrew, and that our Greek Matthew is a translation. Consequently its likeness of wording in the Greek to Mark cannot be explained by its being derived from Mark. For these reasons and others, the Biblical Commission at Rome has rightly ordered Catholics to teach that Matthew was first.

This brings us to the alternative view, that Matthew wrote first, so that Mark's Gospel is really (as St.

* The question of "Q" is discussed later, see pp. 39 ff. ED.

Augustine says) an abbreviation or extract from Matthew, and that lastly Luke used Mark as his principal authority. This view tallies completely with the ancient evidence. It is also fully established, by arguments which I cannot give here, through the internal evidence of the Gospels themselves.*

The evidence for St. Mark's authorship is extraordinarily early and extraordinarily interesting. There is a fragment of St. Papias, preserved by Eusebius. No critic doubts its authenticity. It tells us what was said of St. Mark by the Presbyter or Elder, John, "the disciple of the Lord," whom Papias knew well. It is of no importance here whether this John is or is not the same as the author of the fourth Gospel, whether he is the Apostle or no.† Anyhow he is an aged disciple of Christ, older than Mark, who knows the facts of Our Lord's life, and remembered the writing of the earlier Gospels. Here is what Papias wrote:

"The Elder said this besides: 'Mark, having become the interpreter of Peter, carefully wrote down as much as he related, but not in order, what was spoken or done by the Lord. For he neither heard the Lord nor followed him, but later [followed] Peter, who used to make up his instructions according to the require-

* The internal evidence is fully set out in the author's *Matthew, Mark and Luke* (Longmans, 1937). ED.

† The authorship of St. John's Gospel is discussed below. See pp. 49 ff. ED.

ments, and not as if he was putting together an ordered composition of the Oracles of the Lord. So that
Mark committed no error when he wrote certain things
as he related them. For he had regard to one thing:
to omit nothing of what he heard nor to falsify anything therein.' "

Similar are two other second century accounts. The
first is of Irenaeus, who says that Mark has handed
down to us after St. Peter's death what St. Peter was
preaching at Rome.

Secondly, Clement of Alexandria, at the end of the
second century, tells us as ancient tradition from the
elders: "When Peter publicly preached the Word of
God at Rome, and published the Gospel by the Spirit,
those who were present, being numerous, besought
Mark, as having followed him for many years, and
remembering his words, to write down what he said.
And when Mark had done so, he gave the Gospel to
those who had asked for it. Peter knew of this, and
neither forbade nor encouraged it." Elsewhere Clement tells the story with further detail, when com-
menting on the mention in St. Peter's first Epistle of
"Mark, my son":

"Mark, the follower of Peter, when Peter was publicly preaching the Gospel at Rome in the presence
of certain knights [*equites*], and producing much witness to Christ, at their request, in order that they
might remember what was said, wrote from what

Peter said the Gospel which is called 'according to Mark.' "

Another interesting reference is that of St. Justin martyr, who quotes a passage from St. Mark, who alone relates it, that the sons of Zebedee were called "sons of thunder" by Our Lord. Justin elsewhere describes the Gospels as "memories of the Apostles and those who followed them"; here he quotes this passage as from "the witness of Peter."

After the second century the testimonies are unanimous of early writers such as Tertullian, Origen, Eusebius, Victorinus, Jerome, that Mark wrote what Peter preached at Rome, and the later Fathers and the colophons of manuscripts are similarly unanimous. All this ancient witness is beyond suspicion. If it needed any confirmation, it receives it from an examination of the Gospel itself.

In the first place it was obviously written for Gentiles. It contains little of Our Lord's denunciations of the Pharisees; it explains Jewish customs at length, and translates Aramaic words. But the very use of these Aramaic words shows that the speaker is a Jew. It is a commonplace to add that St. Mark uses Latin words transliterated into Greek, because he wrote at Rome; and some of them look odd enough in Greek letters, such as κεντυρίων (the other Gospels have ἑκατόνταρχος or ἑκατοντάρχης) for *centurio,* ξέστης for *sextans,* αὐλή for *aula.* He explains the Jewish coin λεπτόν by saying that two of them make a *quad-rans*. He even renders *satisfacere* by the two Greek words ἵκανον ποιῆσαι. Another curious note is pecul-iar to Mark: he says that Simon of Cyrene, who car-ried Our Lord's cross, was "the father of Alexander and Rufus." This assumes that his readers were well acquainted with Alexander and Rufus. Now St. Paul's Epistles mention a Rufus at Rome and also an Alex-ander. The coincidence is striking

I have said that very nearly all St. Mark is in St. Matthew. If we compare the two, we find that Mark omits everything in Matthew where Peter was not present. He omits the genealogy and birth of Our Lord, the visit of the Magi, the flight into Egypt— none of this being part of Peter's recollection. But Peter had been a disciple of St. John the Baptist, so we hear of John's preaching and of the Baptism of Christ. But the Temptation of Christ is only men-tioned, the three temptations given at length by Mat-thew and Luke being left out, as Peter was of course not there.

Again, the long discourses given by Matthew are omitted. No doubt most of them were from short-hand reports, which were more common in those days than in modern times. Peter could not remember them by heart entire. He leaves out the whole of the Sermon on the Mount, though he repeats three or four of its proverbial expressions elsewhere. He repeats only a few of Matthew's many parables, adding a very short one. He gives the practical rules given by Our Lord to the Apostles when he sent them out to preach, but omits all the advice. One sermon only can he recall, which is found in chapter 13. It is the prophecy, enormously important to the Apostles, of the destruction of Jerusalem and of the end of the world. In Matthew it is longer, and a whole chapter of three long parables concludes it. But Peter reproduces a great piece, and he explains why: Matthew says Christ made this discourse to his disciples privately; Mark explains that it was Peter and James and John and Andrew who asked him to tell them of the signs of the destruction of the Temple. Thus St. Peter carefully explains why he can repeat this one long discourse from Matthew —because it was an answer to a question of his own.

Another point is very striking. In all the Gospels St. Peter, the chief Apostle, is more prominent than any other. His name occurs about one hundred and twenty times, the next numbers are twenty for Judas Iscariot, twenty for St. John, eighteen for St. James. So St. Peter's name occurs six times as often as that of any other Apostle. St. Mark mentions him often— twenty-five times—but never to his credit. His walking on the sea and the title of "first" are found in Matthew and omitted by Mark. Mark follows Matthew in relating the question of Our Lord "Whom do you say that I am?" but stops at St. Peter's answer "Thou art the Christ," carefully omitting Our Lord's rejoinder "Thou art Peter and upon this rock I will build my Church." He omits the incident of the tribute money, which the Fathers explain in a way specially honourable to Peter. But Mark emphasises the foolishness of St. Peter's remark at the Transfiguration "Let us make here three tabernacles" or tents, "not knowing what he said"; and he adds detail to his denial.

This modesty of St. Peter is emphasised by a comparison with Luke and John. For Luke, following Mark, has not the *Tu es Petrus* so he adds an incident at the Last Supper, where Christ tells Peter that Satan will strive to sift the Apostles as wheat, but that he has prayed that Peter's faith fail not, for it will be Peter's office, after he is converted, to confirm and strengthen his brethren. And St. John adds the restoration of Peter after his three-fold fall, by the three-fold declaration "Thou knowest that I love thee," and the commission to feed Christ's sheep. This notable reticence concerning St. Peter is thus peculiar to St. Mark, and has always been taken as a clear indication that in this Gospel we have not the words of Mark, Peter's admiring disciple, but the recollections of St. Peter himself.

Another peculiarity of this Gospel is its rather disrespectful way of speaking of the Apostles: Our Lord reproves them for not understanding a parable; they do not understand miracles; their heart is hardened;

the sons of Zebedee ask to sit on Christ's right and left—St. Matthew said it was their mother who asked. So St. Peter says of Our Lord: "He looked round with anger"; the people say of him "He is mad" and "Is not this the carpenter?" where Matthew says "the carpenter's son."

The style is diffuse with no literary art; but it is far more vivid than Matthew and Luke, though not in the least dramatic like St. John. The little additions of an eye-witness are often too slight to bear quotation, just as they are too natural to be a sham. Mark describes how Our Lord goes in and out of the house; how the multitude throng; how they crowd into the house, so that there is no room even to eat. He especially describes the amazement of the crowds; he is full of details about the possessed who are cured, and relates at length the tortures and cries caused in them by the devils. One eminently picturesque passage is particularly famous; the effect is entirely lost in the usual English translation. It is a description of the five thousand who were miraculously fed by Our Lord with five loaves:

"And he commanded them to sit down a company here, a company there, upon the green grass (συμπόσια συμπόσια ἐπὶ τῷ χλωρῷ χόρτῳ). And they sat down a flower bed here, a flower bed there, by hundreds and fifties (καὶ ἀνέπεσαν πρασιαὶ πρασιαὶ κατὰ ἑκατὸν καὶ κατὰ πεντήκοντα)." The groups in brilliant Oriental costumes, white with dashes of bright colour, divided by the green of the grass spaces left for the Apostles to walk in as they distributed the bread and fish, looked like "flower beds"—"flower beds" on a green lawn.*

* A question of some interest and importance arises here, the answer to which is not given in the text: If St. Mark's Gospel is—as early tradition asserts and internal evidence indicates—the oral teaching of St. Peter committed to writing by his "interpreter," St. Mark, how are we to account for its remarkable verbal likeness to the Gospel of St. Matthew?

Non-Catholic critics generally reply by denying that our Greek Matthew is substantially identical with the Aramaic original. Without the slightest evidence to support them, they claim that when tradition speaks of St. Matthew's Gospel as the first to be written, this refers only to the lost Aramaic original. The Greek Matthew, they say, is not a mere translation of St. Matthew's Aramaic but a later compilation, and the unknown writer who made it must have used St. Mark's Gospel as a source. They thus consider our Greek Matthew to be dependent on Mark. This view is opposed not only to tradition (which from the earliest times assumes that the Greek Matthew is substantially identical with the Aramaic original) but also to the internal evidence of the Gospels themselves as we have them (as Dom Chapman's *Matthew, Mark and Luke* shows).

Some Catholic scholars seem disposed to compromise with this non-Catholic view by suggesting that, although the Greek Matthew really represents the Aramaic original, yet the translation must have been made after the composition of St. Mark's Gospel and the translator must have used St. Mark's Gospel "to spare him trouble with the dictionary" (Mgr. R. A. Knox in *The Tablet*, 24th July 1943). But it does not seem likely that one who could write the Greek Matthew—"on the whole the best Greek in the New Testament"—would need to take almost his entire vocabulary from a far less competent writer, in all those places where he describes the same incidents.

Dom Chapman, on the other hand, refuses to abandon the unanimous testimony of tradition, which says that St. Matthew's Gospel was the first to be written and always assumes that the Greek version is merely a translation of it. He is therefore able to offer a solution that is not only highly probable in itself but also in complete harmony with all the evidence. He claims that the verbal likeness between the

Of St. Mark himself we hear in the Acts and the
Epistles. Like so many Jews, he had a Roman name,
Marcus, as well as his Jewish name, John; just as
Saul of Tarsus had the Roman name Paulus, and
Joseph Barsabbas was called Justus. He was a cousin
of Barnabas, who had a property in Cyprus, and sold
it, laying the price at the Apostles' feet. The mother
of John Mark was named Mary, and it was to her
house in Jerusalem that St. Peter made his way when
released from prison by an Angel. The Church, we are
told, was assembled there to pray for him, so it was
probably a large house. Ancient tradition says that it
was the same house where Our Lord ate the Passover
and instituted the Blessed Sacrament, and that in the
same upper room on the day of Pentecost the one
hundred and twenty disciples with the Apostles and

---

two Gospels proves that *St. Peter's preaching* (which St. Mark preserves) *was based upon the Greek Matthew.* Thus "Mark is Matthew
conversationally retold by an eye-witness and ear-witness of what Matthew had set down, omitting all parts of Matthew where Peter was not
present, and the long discourses which he would not remember with
exactitude." In brief "Mark appears to be Peter's reading aloud of
Matthew, taken down in shorthand by Mark" (*Matthew, Mark and
Luke,* p. 21; the internal evidence in support of this view is given in
the subsequent pages).

This is the only explanation that harmonizes with all the data. It
accounts for the conversational, diffuse, "redundant" style of St. Mark,
with its characteristic additions of vivid detail such as only an eye-
witness could provide; it accords with the unanimous tradition, supported by internal evidence, that it is St. Peter's preaching that Mark
records; and finally, it explains St. Mark's clear literary dependence
on St. Matthew, which by all tradition was the first Gospel to be
written. Ed.

Our Lady were gathered together. The site on Mount
Sion is now mainly covered by a building revered by
the Mohametans, quite erroneously, as the tomb of
David. One portion of the site, however, where is said
to have been the room in which the Mother of God
died, is now part of the German Benedictine monastery of Mount Sion.

When St. Paul and St. Barnabas went on their first
missionary journey together, they went first to St. Barnabas's home, Cyprus, having John Mark with them,
and St. Paul converted the proconsul of the island.
But when they went on by sea to evangelise Asia
Minor, Mark returned to Jerusalem. He was doubtless quite a young man, for we are told he had not
followed Our Lord nor heard him, presumably being
only a child at the time. When later St. Paul proposed
to St. Barnabas to go on a second journey to visit the
Churches they had founded, St. Barnabas wished to
take Mark again. But St. Paul was angry because Mark
had gone home before, and refused to take him. So
Paul took Silas, or Silvanus, with him to the Asiatic
Churches, leaving Cyprus to Barnabas and Mark. Later
on we find Mark at Rome, when St. Paul had arrived
there as a prisoner. Mark had no doubt been with
St. Peter in the meantime, and St. Paul forgave him.
For he writes to the Colossians from Rome: "Aristar-
chus my fellow prisoner saluteth you, and so doth
Mark, the cousin of Barnabas, touching whom you

have received commandment, if he come unto you receive him." In the letter which was sent to Philemon by the same messenger, St. Paul calls Mark a "fellow-labourer." St. Peter also mentions him at Rome, and it is curious to find Silas or Silvanus again mentioned in the same verses as Mark: "By Silvanus, a faithful brother unto you as I think, I have written briefly. . . . The Church which is in Babylon, elected together with you, saluteth you, and so doth Mark, my son." (The name "Babylon" for Rome occurs also in the Apocalypse.) Later again, St. Paul writes in his last Epistle, the second to Timothy: "Take Mark and bring him with thee, for he is profitable to me for the ministry." Timothy was in Asia, at Ephesus, or at least not far from Troas; so Mark was then also in Asia.

A very ancient tradition tells us that St. Peter sent Mark to found the Church of Alexandria, and this was regarded as certain in the second half of the second century. The bishops of Alexandria, afterwards called Patriarchs and especially Popes, in early times always took the first place after the successors of Peter at Rome, until this prerogative was usurped by the court bishops of Constantinople. The Alexandrian Pope gloried in being the successor of St. Mark, and through him of Peter. Less certain is the legend that St. Mark was martyred at an early date in a popular tumult. His tomb was always venerated at Alexandria, until after the Mohametan conquest the Venetians, who stole so many bodies of saints, carried off as their greatest treasure (about the year 820) the body of St. Mark, who became patron of their state. The Lion of St. Mark was adopted as the ensign of their armies. A curious antique, though not original, account of this pious theft relates that the relics exhaled a sweet odour when dug up from the place before the High Altar of the Church of St. Mark at Alexandria where the Venerable Bede tells us they lay. Therefore, lest the Saracens should examine this sweet-smelling cargo, the Venetians covered the body with pork, and over this a sail, so that when the infidels lifted the sail, they saw the pork which they hated, and held their hands to their noses and departed, crying "Pork, pork!"

The Venetians built for St. Mark the famous Church, covered with precious mosaics, which stands by the side of their Doge's Palace; and since the time of Napoleon it has been the Cathedral of Venice. When one says Mass at the High Altar over the body of St. Mark, as I have often done, if the Gospel of the Mass is from St. Mark, it is the rule to say, not: *Sequentia sancti Evangelii secundum Marcum,* but, with a bow to the Altar: *Sequentia sancti Evangelii secundum istum.* The feast of St. Mark is on April 25th, which is the latest day upon which Easter can fall; this occurs scarcely once in a hundred years.

The Gospel of St. Mark has been less commented on and less quoted than any of the others, not so much because it is the shortest as because it contains so little of Our Lord's discourses. We heard John, "the disciple of the Lord," declaring that the order in Mark was sometimes incorrect, not because Mark made any alteration, but because Peter did not care to keep the chronological order.* The comparison implied cannot be with St. Luke, as St. Luke has exactly preserved the order of St. Mark. It is obvious that the considerable variations from the order of St. Matthew in the first part of Mark are referred to by this ancient authority. St. Matthew very often insists upon the exact order of events, this following that. St. Mark is usually more vague; and we thus find the judgement of John the Presbyter and disciple confirmed by the Gospels themselves; and what is more important, it appears that John regarded Mark as having varied the order of Matthew.

The last twelve verses of Mark are missing in our two oldest manuscripts, and some others mark τέλος, "the end," before them. Eusebius tells us that this was the case in most manuscripts in his time—the beginning of the fourth century. The verses are in all other manuscripts, and are quoted by the writers of the second century. They are accepted by the Church as canonical and inspired. Most non-Catholic critics agree that they are not by St. Mark, and hold that the last page of the Gospel was accidentally lost and a new ending supplied. An Armenian codex gives a curious

* See above, p. 19. ED.

clue: it heads the verses by the words "of Ariston the Elder," presumably meaning Ariston, the presbyter or elder, disciple of the Lord, who was known to Papias and much quoted in Papias's lost work. Hence it is supposed that a lacuna at the end of St. Mark caused by the loss of a page, was supplied by a disciple of the Lord, Ariston or Aristion. This is possible. But the loss of a page implies that there was at the time only one copy of this Gospel. This is too impossible to need any consideration. But there is a break in the sense at this point, and further, it is exactly at this point that the parallel with Matthew and Luke ceases. It seems most likely that at this point St. Peter's lectures ceased, his last lecture being never delivered, owing to some unforeseen circumstance. A finish was supplied. There are strong reasons for thinking it was not St. Mark himself who supplied the conclusion; but there are also strong reasons for thinking that it was St. Mark, for there are very remarkable connexions of wording and sense with the Gospel. And who more than St. Mark was likely to put a finish to his own book?

I recommend the reading of St. Mark's Gospel with the idea of finding in it St. Peter's own descriptions of the life he lived for so short a time in Galilee with the Son of God, whom he loved so passionately. The simplicity of the narrative, its outspokenness and vivacity and warmth, and the obvious originality and unstudied truth give this Gospel an absorbing interest.

The Gospel of St. Luke

ST. LUKE IS THE AUTHOR of a work in two volumes, the Gospel called by his name and its continuation, the Acts of the Apostles. He begins each with a preface, addressed to a certain Theophilus, who is usually supposed to have been a Christian of high rank, as he is called κράτιστος, which is something like "Right Honourable" or "Your Excellency"; but it is also possible that "Theophilus," "friend of God," simply means any Christian.

The usual attempts have been made by "liberal" critics to show that both these books are late compilations, partly based on earlier sources. The most obvious reply to these critics is the fact that one style throughout both books forces us to conclude that both are throughout by one author. This is shown convincingly, in the first place, by St. Luke's vocabulary and by his use of certain favourite words throughout his writings. It is true that in reproducing sayings of Our Lord which are also in Matthew and Mark, he gives them almost without alteration. But the narrative is always rewritten in his own style, easily recognisable by his vocabulary. Every reasonable critic must admit that both Gospel and Acts are by one author.

Another point is suggested by the expression used by St. Paul in his Epistle to the Colossians: "Luke the beloved physician." It has been shown by Hobart that Luke's frequent mentions of sicknesses are couched in more correct medical language than in the other Gospels, and that his two prefaces are modelled on those of famous medical treatises.

Another peculiarity of style is his imitation of the Septuagint, the ancient Greek translation of the Old Testament. Instead of the Aramaisms which are frequent in the other Gospels, of which Luke has some from his sources, he has a number of habitual Hebraisms borrowed, not from the Hebrew, but from the Greek Septuagint. The most obvious of these is ἐγένετο δὲ, "and it came to pass that." Everyone recognises this as characteristic of the Old Testament. It is not a Greek expression. It occurs only six times in Matthew, four times in Mark, never in John; but forty-two times in Luke, as well as twenty-one times in Acts. It is clear from this biblical style which St. Luke alone affects among New Testament writers, that he must have meant his books to be read in church together with the Old Testament. This is supported by his care that everything throughout his Gospel should be edifying and easily understood. Some startling paradoxes and exaggerations in Our Lord's own

words are toned down by St. Luke or omitted—such
as the saying about casting a mountain into the sea,
or suggestions that Our Lord was angry or troubled
or groaned. He avoids, out of reverence, mentioning
that men said Our Lord was mad. Especially he reveres
the Apostles, and glosses over their early ignorance
and want of understanding as far as he can. In the
other three Gospels, of Matthew, Peter and John, the
authors, being themselves Apostles, are quite ready to
point out their shortcomings. Luke could not omit the
denial of St. Peter, but he explained previously that
St. Peter was to be converted. But that the Apostles
strove who should be the greatest, that James and
John wished to have the first places in the Kingdom,
that Peter rebuked Our Lord, and that Christ said to
him "Get thee behind me, Satan"—these and many
smaller points, which threw discredit on the Apostles,
are omitted by Luke with evident care. He shows the
same reverence for the Apostles in Acts, though he is
ready to suggest imperfection in Barnabas and Mark,
who were but disciples like himself.

Everyone knows how St. Luke, though never nam-
ing himself in Acts, yet points out where he was present by the use of the first person plural "we." We
thus learn of his journeys with St. Paul, and how
eventually he accompanied him to Jerusalem, whence
St. Paul was sent to Caesarea to save him from the
Jews, and was kept in prison there for two years. It

would seem that St. Luke remained at Caesarea all this time; for when Paul appealed to Caesar, and was sent as a prisoner to Rome by sea, he was accompanied on the ship by Luke and Aristarchus, who shared the shipwreck, and arrived together with the Apostle at Rome, and lived with him there for two years, awaiting his trial. So ends the book of Acts.

This is a strange ending. It is quite incomprehensible that any book should finish in this unfinished way, except because the author was suddenly interrupted and the work left incomplete. But Acts does not seem to be incomplete. Consequently we naturally assume that it ends where it does end simply because there was nothing more to say: in other words, that St. Luke has carried the story right up to the moment of writing. Hence we get the date of the completion of Acts —the second year of St. Paul's imprisonment at Rome, about 62, when he was still living with a soldier to guard him, in his own hired house, uncertain of the date of his long-postponed trial.

This is the obvious date, and the traditional date. It has proved very annoying to "liberal" critics, and to conservative critics like Zahn, or Plummer, who wish to show that they are not obscurantists by dating St. Luke's Gospel after the siege of Jerusalem. The best way of getting out of their difficulty was Ramsay's suggestion that St. Luke had planned a third volume, which should contain St. Paul's trial and what happened afterwards—probably his acquittal, his further journeys to Asia and to Spain, with a return to Rome and martyrdom. Only St. Luke is supposed to have been unable to write this book. However, as tradition says that he lived to the age of eighty-six, he might well have had time. The hypothesis is gratuitous. Harnack has argued very forcibly that the last seven chapters of Acts lead us up to St. Paul's trial: the prophecy of Agabus, the farewell to the priests of Ephesus at the port of Miletus, who sorrowed that they would see St. Paul no more, the riot at Jerusalem, and night escort to Caesarea, the long imprisonment there and the trial before Agrippa, the voyage to Rome with shipwreck and escape—all leads up to the trial before Nero. The reader is anxious to know how it will turn out, and he is left, like the Apostle, waiting at Rome without further news. No one could have written a book up to such a futile though tantalising result, except because nothing further had occurred, and the delay seemed likely to continue.

As a fact, St. Paul seems to have been mistaken when he told the priests of Ephesus that they would see his face no more. We learn from the second Epistle to Timothy that the Apostle had been again to Ephesus, as he had left a cloak there and books, which he asks to be sent on to him at Rome.

St. Luke had plenty of time during the two years he lived with St. Paul at Rome to write the book of

Acts. The date of his Gospel is earlier. He may have written it in his first year at Rome, or before this while St. Paul was in prison for two years at Caesarea, or even earlier yet. One reason for thinking he wrote it at Rome might be that St. Mark's Gospel was written there, and that it was at Rome that he became acquainted with it, and used it for his principal authority, as containing the recollections of the Prince of the Apostles. But he must have collected the materials which are peculiar to him before he left Palestine.

The preface to the Gospel of St. Luke tells us why he wrote: "Because many have made attempts to recount a narration of the things which have been fulfilled amongst us, according as they have been handed down to us by those who were from the beginning eyewitnesses and ministers of the Word, it seemed good to me also, in that I have followed up all these matters carefully from the start, to write them one after another for Your Excellency, Theophilus, that you may know the certitude as to the words in which you have been instructed."

We learn from this that several persons had attempted to write in Greek, none of them being eyewitnesses or original teachers. The chief of these is evidently Mark, who wrote only a partial Gospel, with no account of Our Lord's Birth from a Virgin or of his early life, with scarcely any of his discourses, and with an incomplete story of the Resurrection, since

Luke did not use the last twelve verses of Mark. What other sources had Luke? We know none of them. Some of his information may have been taken from written documents; the rest was gathered by Luke himself from the recollections of eye-witnesses.

But the two-thirds of St. Mark which make up the skeleton of St. Luke supply not quite half his matter. Half of the other half—that is, a quarter of the whole —is parallel to various bits of St. Matthew. The rest —more than a quarter—is peculiar to St. Luke.

The part common to Matthew and Luke, but not in Mark, is known as "Q," and modern critics suppose it to be from a written Greek source of early date, probably older than St. Mark, and known to him. The passages in question are merely bits of discourses, dispersed here and there. They are often spoken of as "the Logia," and are supposed by "liberal" critics to be the original St. Matthew: a collection of sayings of Christ, without incidents except the Baptism and Temptation and one miracle, with no account of his Birth or Passion. St. Mark has been supposed to have written his Gospel of incidents to supplement this small book of discourses, "Q"; while the author of Matthew, and St. Luke, each independently combined Mark and "Q" into one book, together with some independent traditions. This, of course, contradicts the tradition that Matthew was the first Gospel and was written in Hebrew.

But "Q" is by no means homogeneous, and could never have existed as a book, and detailed examination shows that many bits of it will not square with the theory for various reasons. I can give here only the general fact, which is conclusive as it stands: the bits termed "Q" have three totally different characters.

First, there are passages where the event or the discourse is clearly the same in Matthew and Luke, but so wholly different in wording that the two cannot be from the same Greek source, and so different in nature that they are obviously independent reports of the same event or sermon. This is the case with the sixth chapter of St. Luke, known as "the Sermon on the Plain." It is the same discourse as St. Matthew's Sermon on the Mount, but a much less complete report. The same appears to be true of the "Woes" to the Scribes and Pharisees, shorter in Luke, and seldom agreeing in the actual Greek words. There are many less noticeable examples. These bits cannot belong to a Greek source "Q" used by both evangelists.

Secondly, there are bits where Matthew and Luke are the same, word for word, or with here and there a favourite word introduced by St. Luke. If we compare these bits with the "triple tradition" where the three Synoptists are parallel, we find that in the "triple tradition" St. Luke is not so like St. Matthew, nor even so like St. Mark, whom he is directly using. It therefore becomes absurd to suppose that in these passages attributed to "Q" where Matthew and Luke are exactly alike in words, they have both copied a common source exactly; it is obvious that one used the other directly, else the likeness would have been merely what we find when Mark is the mean between the two.

Thirdly, there are at least three remarkable passages where the two former phenomena are combined: the parable of the talents or pounds, the parable of the feast, and the story of the centurion's servant. These are quite differently told by the two evangelists, but yet the spoken sentences are reported in exactly the same words. I instance the centurion. In Matthew the centurion comes to Christ, in Luke he sends his friends; in the whole narrative the Greek words are different. But the centurion's words—"Lord, I am not worthy, etc."—are exactly the same in both, and so is Our Lord's comment—"I have not found such faith in Israel."

The explanation of this is obvious: St. Luke possessed a more complete account of the miracle than he found in St. Matthew, and he writes it down; but the words of the centurion and of Christ were better reported in St. Matthew, so he copies them into his account.

A confirmation of this is curious: St. Matthew always calls the servant $\pi\alpha\tilde{\iota}\varsigma$, whereas St. Luke uses the word $\delta o\tilde{\upsilon}\lambda o\varsigma$; but in giving the words "Speak the

word only and my servant shall be healed," St. Luke
uses Matthew's word παῖς.

Now it seems perfectly clear that when St. Luke
was composing his Gospel he possessed no complete
translation of St. Matthew; but it seems equally clear
that before it was finished he came to know our Greek
St. Matthew, and that he revised many parts of his
Gospel according to the wording of this translation,
but not any of those parts which he had taken from
St. Mark, evidently being aware that St. Mark's
authority, St. Peter, had used St. Matthew, so that
St. Luke prefers St. Mark to St. Matthew. He also must
have introduced here and there short pieces from
Matthew, but was unable to interpolate much into his
nearly complete manuscript.

I have said that St. Luke respects the order of St.
Mark. In fact he inserts his additional matter into
St. Mark in great chunks, and never in small details.
He has a long piece at the beginning on Our Lord's
Birth, and a long piece at the end about his Resurrection. Of the other additions, the longest is an interpolation of scarcely less than nine chapters at about
the end of St. Mark's ninth chapter. All this gives a
series of incidents and discourses and parables, described as taking place during Our Lord's last journey
to Jerusalem. There does not seem to be any strict
chronological order either here or elsewhere in St.
Luke. He often strings together incidents with only

vague indications of time, and hangs one saying on another without any logical connexion.

The extraordinary beauty of St. Luke's Gospel depends chiefly on those parts, more than a quarter of the whole, which are in no other Gospel.

Of these portions the most famous and the most dearly loved by all Christians is that which comprises his first and second chapters. This portion contains the story of Zachary and Elizabeth, and his wonderful narrative of the Annunciation, known to the Middle Ages as "the Golden Gospel." Next the birth of St. John the Baptist, and then (in the second chapter) the Nativity of Jesus in a stable and the appearance of the Angel to the shepherds and their adoration of the Divine Babe. Then come the Presentation in the Temple and Simeon and Anna, and the Finding of Jesus in the Temple. With these incomparable stories come the three Canticles of the New Testament: the *Benedictus,* the *Magnificat,* and the *Nunc Dimittis.* Ancient tradition says that St. Luke was a painter as well as a physician. At all events these two chapters of his have inspired more great artists than have any other writings.

Next in importance are St. Luke's unequalled series of parables. Besides those he has borrowed from St. Mark, he alone has those lessons of love of our neighbour and of the poor—the Good Samaritan, the Rich Man and Lazarus, the Unjust Steward—those lessons of prayer like the Unjust Judge, and above all those most touching of all stories about the love of God for sinners—the Pharisee and the Publican, and the Prodigal Son, the Lost Drachma and the Lost Sheep.

If we add to these parables St. Luke's beautiful story of the feast in the house of Simon the Pharisee, when the woman that was a sinner washed Our Lord's feet with her tears, the story of Zacchaeus, the prince of publicans, the little rich man who climbed into a sycamore, and again the repentance and forgiveness of the Good Thief by Our Lord as he hung on the cross, we shall realize why St. Luke is "the Gospel of the Saviour" and forgiveness.

Again, the story of the woman who washed Our Lord's feet, the miracle of the bent woman, the feast of Mary and Martha, the woman who cried out from the crowd "Blessed is the womb that bore thee," and all that is said about Anna and Elizabeth and Our Blessed Lady—all this has obtained for St. Luke the name of "the Gospel of the Holy Women."

"The Gospel of the Disciples" is another name, for St. Luke tells us of the sending out of the seventy-two disciples, and gives the tale of the two disciples who walked to Emmaus on the first Easter-day.

St. Luke alone tells us how Christ was brought before Herod. St. John had not penetrated into Herod's palace as he did into the house of the High Priest. Perhaps this account came to St. Luke from

Joanna, the wife of Herod's steward, whom St. Luke alone mentions among the women who followed Our Lord from Galilee and ministered to him of their substance. Or he may have learnt it from Manaen, the foster-brother of Herod, whom he must have known at Antioch.

Finally, St. Luke alone tells us of the Angel who appeared to Our Lord in his Agony in the Garden, of Our Lord's prayer "Father, forgive them for they know not what they do," and of his last cry "Father, into thy hands I commend my spirit."

Thus all these additions of St. Luke are of astonishing beauty. How painfully he must have collected them, and how carefully and wisely selected them!

We can now guess why he omitted a third part of St. Mark, whose Gospel he evidently venerated and wished to complete. What he omitted would not be lost, since it was in St. Mark. But he had so much to add of infinite value to souls. And he is evidently anxious not to exceed a single volume. For there was a definite size for a roll of commerce, and St. Luke has reached the limit of custom and convenience. His is the longest book in the New Testament, and the publishers and booksellers would have allowed no more. And when we examine what St. Luke has omitted of St. Mark, we can almost invariably guess the reason. In most cases it is a duplicate which he omits. For example, he leaves out the supper at

Bethany where Mary anointed Our Lord's head, because he has another banquet where a sinner washes his feet. He leaves out the feeding of the four thousand, because that of the five thousand suffices. He leaves out one storm out of two, and so forth. And speaking of storms, let us note that the other Gospels speak of the fresh-water lake of Tiberias, where Peter and John fished, as "the sea." But St. Luke had frequently been on the real salt sea with St. Paul, and he calls this inland piece of water a "lake" and never a "sea"!

Let us ask St. Luke for the love of prayer, of which he speaks more than the other Gospels, for the love of our neighbour and especially of the poor, of whom he says so much, for sorrow for sin and confidence in the mercy of Jesus Christ, which he teaches in so touching a manner. And let us ask him for devotion to the Mother of God, of whom he tells us most. For to St. Luke we owe the Angelical Salutation, the "Hail Mary."

The Gospel of St. John

CRITICS ARE FOND of telling us that St. John's Gospel is an amazing document, because it is so very unlike the others. In reality the amazing fact is rather that the others are so much alike. The fourth Gospel was written some forty years after St. Luke's. It is a supplement by the last survivor of the Apostles.

Occasionally St. John repeats what was already in the other Gospels. The most prominent example of this is the miracle of the feeding of the five thousand, followed by Our Lord's walking on the sea. This was in all three of the other Gospels. St. John tells the story of the supper at Bethany again, which only Luke had omitted. The whole history of the Passion and Resurrection is related afresh, with some omissions (such as the Agony in the Garden) and much new detail.

But St. John assumes that his readers know the earlier Gospels. Just as Mark begins where Peter's memories began, with the witness to Christ by John the Baptist, so does St. John.

He supposes that his readers know from Matthew and Luke the circumstances of Our Lord's Birth from a Virgin, and that God alone is his Father. He says much of St. John the Baptist's witness to Christ, repeating the very words of the other Gospels and adding to them, but assuming the Baptism of Our Lord, not relating it. In the same way he tells us how after the Last Supper Our Lord washes his disciples' feet, and makes more definite the revelation then made of the treachery of Judas; but he says not a word of the Institution of the Holy Eucharist, for this was in the other three Gospels and in an Epistle of St. Paul, besides being known to every Christian by weekly if not daily experience. He assumes that the reader knows St. Luke; for when he tells again the story of the supper at Bethany from Matthew and Mark, he explains (what they do not say) that Lazarus and his sisters were present, and adds the detail that "Martha served." This detail would have no meaning to anyone who did not know St. Luke's story of Martha's being gently reproved for taking too much trouble in serving. Similarly he gives further information about details which are only in St. Mark. The latter says that the Apostles ironically remarked that it would take "two hundred pennyworth" of bread to feed the five thousand men; St. John explains that it was Philip who said this. St. Matthew says the disciples grumbled at the waste, when the box of precious spikenard was broken over Our Lord's head, pointing out that it should have been sold for the poor. St. Mark tells us they said it should have been sold for "three hundred pence." St. John explains that it was Judas Iscariot who made the estimate of three hundred pence, and this, not because he cared for the poor, but because he kept the common purse and was a thief.

References to St. Matthew are less noticeable, but certain. In some passages St. John's wording seems to show that he had all the three Synoptic Gospels before him.

Modern critics were at one time very determined that the fourth Gospel was a late compilation of the second century, even of the end of that century. Conservative critics have so persistently argued that actual testimony, scarcely disputed in any point, abundantly forces it back out of this century, that the "liberals" have had to admit that it can be not later than its traditional date—about 97 or possibly earlier.

They have, however, denied that it is by the same author as the Epistles of St. John; and Wellhausen, the famous Higher Critic of the Old Testament, in his old age pointed out a number of slight inconsistencies or breaks in the narrative which proved, in his opinion, that it is a compilation consisting of a *Grundschrift* or original document, altered and added to by a series of editors. This absolutely idiotic theory—I think no milder word will suit it—passes over the fact that the style of St. John in Gospel and Epistles is so easily recognisable and unique, that one could identify almost any individual verse taken alone as being by him. It is imitable, no doubt, for it is extraordinarily simple, with hardly any subordinate clauses, except with ὅς, ἵνα or ὅτι. But an ancient interpolator would not have imitated it—it is a thing ancient interpolators never did. Moreover if St. John's style could be imitated, his matter could not. It has a beauty and depth of its own, which are beyond the power of a copyist to invent. The notion of older critics that the first Epistle is spurious, and a mere forgery in a carefully imitative style, is so extremely silly that the best answer to it is to ask the critic to try and write another chapter of the Epistle, which will be accepted as worthy of it.

It is not as if there were not real literary difficulties about St. John. There is a famous passage of the Gospel—the story of the woman taken in adultery—which is not in St. John's easily recognisable style. It is also absent in a great many manuscripts, and was not accepted by some ancient writers. It is, however, neatly fitted into its position. It is not an awkward interpolation. It is accepted by the Church as canonical.

We know that St. Paul dictated his letters. We are told that St. Peter depended upon St. Mark as his interpreter. We see that the two Epistles of St. Peter differ considerably in style, doubtless because written down for him by different scribes. The same seems to be true in St. John's case. The evidence of Justin and

Irenaeus concerning St. John's authorship of the Apocalypse is very strong, and this is confirmed by its free use by Papias, a disciple of St. John. Both Gospel and Apocalypse are thus vouched for as by John the Apostle by unexceptionable witnesses. Yet their style is very different. The vocabulary of the Apocalypse resembles that of St. Paul, as though St. John's amanuensis was an Ephesian who knew St. Paul's Epistles well. A great deal of imagery is borrowed from Daniel, and still more from Ezechiel. Yet doctrines and peculiarities are found in the Apocalypse which suggest the same author as that of the Gospel; and no one denies that in many ways the Apocalypse is very near the Gospel. And there is a vigour and picturesqueness which cannot be paralleled in the New Testament except in the fourth Gospel.

For the chief literary characteristic of the fourth Gospel is not the simplicity of its language, its smoothness, gentleness and sweetness, but its extraordinary dramatic vividness. Its character-drawing is surprising. It is full of dialogue. In Our Lord's discourses, the individual Apostles, the Jews, or the Pharisees interrupt and argue; there are dialogues with the woman of Samaria, with Nicodemus, with Pilate. And the truth to life is as often comedy as tragedy. Both appear in the story of the woman taken in adultery, and who could have told the story but St. John? It seems to be an afterthought, even later than his twenty-first chapter, and written down by a different scribe—very likely Papias—and inserted where we find it by the Apostle's own direction.

The internal evidence of authorship is very remarkable.

In the first place, it is perfectly clear that the author is not a Greek-speaking convert of the second generation of Christians. He is a Jew, whose style is full of Semitisms, whose knowledge of Jewish customs and habits is thorough. Further, he is a Jew of Palestine, who knows the country, and was familiar with Jerusalem before its destruction, though he writes much later. All these points have been worked out in detail by commentators.

Secondly, the Gospel was not an anonymous work, for it not only claims to be by a very close disciple who was an eye-witness of the events it narrates, but appeals to his veracity by such phrases as "He that hath seen it, hath borne witness, and his witness is true, and he knoweth that he saith the truth, that you also may believe." There is no meaning in these celebrated attestations, unless they are addressed to readers who know the writer's credentials. Besides, the textual evidence that the title has always been "according to John" is alone perfectly satisfactory.

Thirdly, there is curious evidence that the writer's name was John, and that he was the only John among the more important disciples. His Gospel has much about St. John the Baptist, yet he is never mentioned as "John the Baptist" as in the other Gospels, but simply as "John." The former evangelists say "the Baptist" to distinguish him from John the Apostle. But the fourth Gospel does not need to make the distinction, for the Baptist is the only John besides the writer. This would be less noteworthy, were it not that the fourth Gospel is particularly careful about distinctions. There were two Simons among the Apostles, and though Simon the Canaanite is never mentioned by St. John, the other Simon is always called by the double name "Simon Peter." Similarly, two of the Apostles were called Judas, and the fourth Gospel always calls the traitor "Judas Iscariot, the son of Simon" and the other is "Judas, not the Iscariot."

Fourthly, the writer of the Gospel calls himself "the disciple whom Jesus loved," and then again "the other disciple." It is admitted that the writer is the unnamed disciple who was invited, together with Andrew, to "come and see" where Christ was dwelling, at the beginning of the Gospel. He describes himself as leaning on Our Lord's breast at the Last Supper and being urged by Peter to ask who was the traitor. He says he was at the foot of the cross, and that Jesus commended his Mother to his care, and that he saw blood and water flow from the pierced side. He describes himself as running with Peter to the empty tomb. He is one of the disciples who is present at the miraculous draught of fishes, and to him Peter says "It is the Lord" whom he sees on the shore; and after they have dined, and Peter's martyrdom has been predicted by Christ, Peter turns and says "What shall this man do?" seeing his friend. And so the Gospel ends: "This is the disciple who is witness of these things and wrote these things."

Who is this disciple? The answer is plain enough, by mere statistics. Yet critics have been found to say, and the opinion has even been popular since Hugo Delff's hypothesis was approved by the late Dr. Sanday, that the beloved disciple who wrote the fourth Gospel, was not John the Apostle, but another John, so young that he could be present with the Twelve at the Last Supper and not be counted—probably that "John the Presbyter" who in his old age was known to Papias.

Now this suggestion is contradicted by the argument I have just explained, that "John" in this Gospel always means the Baptist. A second proof is that in the other three Gospels, excluding the lists of the Apostles, John the Apostle is mentioned seventeen times and his brother James fifteen times, besides three mentions of "the sons of Zebedee." Compare the fact that Judas Iscariot is mentioned only nine times, and no other Apostle more than four times. But the fourth Gospel is far more communicative about individual

Apostles, mentioning Philip twelve times, Thomas eight times, Andrew five times; yet it never mentions the two who were next in importance after Peter, that is to say, James and John, except once by saying "the sons of Zebedee," thus assuming that the reader knows perfectly well that these were James and John. Hence, when we ask who is "the beloved disciple," it is obvious that he is either James or John—and nobody supposes he was James.

A third argument is this: every time "the beloved disciple" is mentioned, it is with Peter—except at the foot of the cross. We ask: "What disciple was Peter's close companion?" Again the answer is easy. In the other Gospels we find that Zebedee and his sons, James and John, were partners with Peter and Andrew. Next we find that Jesus kept three disciples close to himself—Peter and James and John—who were taken into the house of Jairus to see the cure of his little daughter, who alone were present at the Transfiguration and at Our Lord's Agony in the Garden. Further, it was Peter and John who were sent to prepare the Passover, and St. Peter himself, in St. Mark's Gospel, mentions John more often than the other Synoptists do. In the first part of Acts, where Peter is the chief speaker and actor in the foundation of the Church at Jerusalem, Peter and John are always together, and the formula "Peter and John" occurs seven times. If we turn to the fourth Gospel, what can be more clear than that the beloved disciple, who is always with Peter, is the Apostle John?

From every point of view, therefore, it is quite clear that the writer of the fourth Gospel intends the reader to understand that he, the disciple whom Jesus loved, is John the Apostle. If we prefer to say that the Gospel is a forgery, then it remains clear that the forger intended to be taken for the Apostle. Only then we are met by the consideration that many points in the arguments I have used are too subtle for a forger to have used—apart from the consideration that a forger would hardly be able to pretend so successfully to knowledge of Jewish customs and of Palestinian geography before the Jewish war, and would hardly be likely to write so lofty and inspired a book!

All this internal evidence is in exact accordance with the convincing external evidence from the second century, that the fourth Gospel is a whole, not a compilation, and that it is by the Apostle John, who was really a witness, as he claims, of all that he relates.

Thus the two friends, Peter and John, have bequeathed to us two Gospels, the second and the fourth, which are personal reminiscences, with nothing at second hand.

Matthew and Luke, from witnesses whom they knew, described the human Birth of Christ from his Virgin Mother; St. John assumes all this, and will not add to it, as he is only giving his own witness;

but he puts instead the statement of the Divine and Eternal Birth of the Son of God from his Heavenly Father: "In the beginning was the Word, and the Word was with God, and the Word was God." This is the programme of the whole Gospel, described more fully in that longer introduction which we call St. John's first Epistle. "The Life was manifested," he says, and he, John, had seen this divine life lived on earth in human flesh: "We have seen and do bear witness, and declare unto you the life eternal, which was with the Father, and hath appeared unto us; that which we have seen and heard we declare to you, that you also may have fellowship with us." And similarly, at the end of his Gospel (though before the last chapter, which is an afterthought) he explains why he wrote:

"Many other signs also did Jesus, which are not written in this book; but these are written that you may believe that Jesus is the Christ, the Son of God, and that believing you may have life in his name."

When St. John wrote, about the year 97, heretics had arisen, and he, the last Apostle, denounced them, and set down his witness against the Docetae, and Cerinthus, and the Nicolaitans. He has two opposite errors to meet: the denial by the Judaizers of the Divinity of Christ, and by the Docetae of the reality of his Human Nature, which they thought was but a phantom. (We find the same heresies combated scarcely ten years later in the letters of St. Ignatius of Antioch.)

Hence the reality of Our Lord's Crucifixion is testified with great solemnity by the blood and water from his side: "He that saw it bore witness, and he knoweth that his witness is true." And this is repeated in the Epistle. The reality of the bodily Resurrection is vouched for by the doubt of St. Thomas, who touched the wounds of Christ and believed.

On the other hand, no less than five chapters—the fifth, seventh, eighth, tenth and twelfth—are mainly filled with Our Lord's teaching, chiefly at Jerusalem, often in the Temple, that he is the Son of God, while the Jews interrupt and argue. A few great miracles are told in detail: besides the feeding of the five thousand and the walking on the sea, which are repeated from the other Gospels, there are the changing of water into wine at Cana, the healing of the ruler's son, the miracle at the Pool of Bethsaida, the cure of the man blind from his birth, and the raising of Lazarus.

But these signs are not merely chosen because more than other miracles they prove the Divinity of Christ, but for special reasons. The raising of the dead Lazarus is given as the chief cause of the hatred of the chief Priests, who feared that the new Messiah would lead the people into riots, which would bring on a complete conquest by the Romans. The story of the blind man, and the way he scores off the Pharisees is intended to cast ridicule on these hypocrites. I wish it were possible to quote it in full, to show the effective and amusing manner in which St. John relates their discomfiture, and then suddenly turns to the solemn and touching confession of the man who was cured. The evangelist, like Shakespeare, moves us by the sharp changes from laughter to tears. Then the long instruction on the Holy Eucharist, the Bread of Life, in the sixth chapter, rests upon the preceding miracles of the multiplication of the loaves and fishes, and the bodily walking on the water, indicating that there is no impossibility of the feeding of all Christians throughout the world and throughout the ages on the Flesh of the Son of Man, the Flesh which could ascend to Heaven, where he was before. (Another sacramental discourse is that on Baptism and the new birth, to Nicodemus.)

But more noticeable still, as a contrast to the Synoptic Gospels, which follow St. Matthew in giving mainly the public teaching to the crowds of Galilee, is the teaching as to the union of the Christian with Christ which fills the fourteenth, fifteenth, sixteenth and seventeenth chapters—the chapters which contain the discourses after the Last Supper. Here we find the detailed promise of the coming of the Holy Ghost to teach and strengthen, the promise to which St. Luke had referred, and the doctrine of the indwelling of Christ, the union with him as the branches with the

Vine. This had been, indeed, the chief doctrine of St. Paul in his Epistles, and modern critics tell us that the fourth Gospel is Pauline. They hold that the first three Gospels contain a development of the real teaching of Jesus of Nazareth, though they do not agree what that original teaching was; that St. Paul developed it still further, inventing the Christian religion as we know it, and the organised Church; and that later on, the fourth Gospel carries on this doctrine in a more mystical manner.

But both St. Paul and St. John claim, and surely with sincerity, that they teach nothing but what Jesus of Nazareth himself taught. Each of them is overflowing with love and gratitude to Jesus, each believes he is a true disciple.

But it is perhaps more striking to notice the identity of doctrine under a complete dissimilarity of language. There are four verses in St. John's first chapter in which he seems to betray acquaintance with St. Paul's Epistles, which, indeed, he must have known. But they are the words of the evangelist, not of Christ; and nowhere else does he show any parallel whatever to St. Paul's language. This is the only passage where he uses the word χάρις, *gratia*, "grace"; he never uses the word πίστις, "faith." He teaches the same doctrine of our union with Christ that St. Paul does, but in a different way, from a different point of view, and in totally different language. Nothing can be plainer than that John has not borrowed from Paul. We have two independent testimonies, both perfectly candid, truthful, enthusiastic and insistent, to a common doctrine that must have come, as they both declare it did, from Christ himself.

I cannot dwell on the differences between St. John and the Synoptic Gospels. He certainly intends to correct certain impressions which readers of them might gather. The most important is as to the length of Our Lord's public ministry. From the Synoptists we might have supposed it lasted less than one year. They relate only one visit to Jerusalem—that for the last Passover. They begin their story only after St. John the Baptist has been shut up in prison. But St. John mentions several feasts, and probably makes the public ministry last two and a half or even three and a half years. He points out half way through his Gospel that the Baptist was not yet imprisoned, assuming that we know of his imprisonment from the other Gospels.

There is the famous question whether St. John sets the Crucifixion on the day of the Passover, the day on which the lambs were killed, and not on the day following, as the Synoptists appear to do. The question has been fought between Easterns and Westerns —for the Easterns use leavened bread for the Holy Eucharist, and wish to show that the Last Supper was just before the days of unleavened bread—and between Catholics and Catholics, and between critics and critics. That most brilliant scholar and most fervent defender of the Church, the late Monsignor Duchesne, used to say that when he was a young man he imagined, like many young scholars, that he had discovered an infallible way of reconciling St. John here with the Synoptists, but that in later years he had realised that we are too ignorant of the customs of those days to assert any of the many solutions to be decisive! *

The extreme contrast between the writings of St. Paul and St. John depends on their likeness in one point: the way their own personality pierces through in all that they write. St. Paul's self throbs with life in his Epistles, his earnestness, his enthusiasm, his intense sensitiveness. Similarly, yet in great contrast, the extraordinary genius of St. John catches hold of us in every verse, and this in two ways. First, there is the astonishing simplicity of the style. St. Luke tells us that Peter and John were uneducated: ἀγράμματοι καὶ ἰδιῶται; but St. John was then young, and in the sixty years more that passed before he wrote his Gospel he must have lived with many men of high education, both Jews and Gentiles. But he dictates in short sentences with simple words; his constructions are babyish, or have the simplicity of a very old man. He possesses a style which seems at first a hopelessly imperfect instrument of expression. Parts of the first

* For an interesting discussion of this question the reader is referred to the first essay in *Men and Manners in the Days of Christ* by J. P. Arendzen (Sheed and Ward). ED.

Epistle are like a child's first reading book, admirable for a first Greek primer. But, in the second place, if you read it thoughtfully, you do not ask for the splendid *sesquipedalia verba* of Aeschylus or Shakespeare, for the rhythms of Cicero and the long waving periods of Hooker or Ruskin, but you feel that the unadorned, brief thoughts, with their strange repetitions, are more impressive, and more moving, more worthy of the deepest and most divine thoughts than any human eloquence could be. And you turn to the varied dialogue in the Gospel, and you find it is lifelike, just because it is unstudied; and you turn to the narrative, and you find that the short words and plain phrases are capable of unsurpassed dramatic effects, as in the raising of Lazarus. The apparent inadequacy of the means enhances the result. Do you know how a woodcut by Holbein can sometimes give the effect of brilliant light and almost of colour by a mere outline? So I think it is with St. John—*simplex munditiis*. For he was both the "son of thunder" and the "disciple whom Jesus loved."

There are some ancient tales of St. John's life at Ephesus. Particularly beautiful is the story of the young man who joined a band of robbers and was brought back by the Apostle.* We also read that he

This story is told at some length by Clement of Alexandria. The young man was converted by St. John, who on leaving Ephesus entrusted him to the care of the bishop. Many years later, when the Apostle returned, he learned that his former convert had fallen into had a pet partridge which he used to fondle, saying that "the bow cannot always be bent." Finally St. Jerome tells us that when St. John was so old that he had to be carried to the Church by his disciples and could only speak a few words, Sunday after Sunday he would say only: "Little children, love one another." And his disciples grew tired of hearing always the same words, and said: "Master, why do you always speak in this way?" And he gave an answer worthy of John: "Because it is the Lord's precept, and if this alone is performed, it is enough."

---

bad company and was now the leader of a band of brigands in the neighbourhood. Calling immediately for a horse, St. John set off in pursuit of the renegade. When at last he found him, he entreated him with great earnestness to abandon his wicked life, assuring him that there was still hope of his salvation if only he would repent, and even declaring his readiness to give up his own life to save the other's soul. The man was so moved that he cast aside his weapons, fell on his knees and burst into tears. Whereupon St. John took his hand and kissed it, and then led him back to the assembled brethren. ED.

Appendix

Documents Relating to the Four Gospels

I. TESTIMONY OF THE EARLY FATHERS

(1) St. Papias, Bishop of Hierapolis (c. 130), described by St. Irenaeus as "a hearer of John and the associate of Polycarp," writes as follows:

"[John] the Elder said this besides: 'Mark, having become the interpreter of Peter, carefully wrote down as much as he related, but not in order, what was spoken or done by the Lord. For he neither heard the Lord nor followed him, but later [followed] Peter, who used to make up his instructions according to the requirements, and not as if he was putting together an ordered composition of the Oracles of the Lord. So that Mark committed no error when he wrote certain things as he related them. For he had regard to one thing: to omit nothing of what he heard nor to falsify anything therein' . . . Matthew wrote the Oracles [of the Lord] in the Hebrew tongue, and everyone interpreted them as best he could" (Quoted by Eusebius in his *Ecclesiastical History*, III:39).

(2) St. Irenaeus, who was born and educated in Asia and finally became Bishop of Lyons (c. 185), was a disciple of St. Polycarp who was a disciple of

St. John. His witness is, therefore, of very great value. In his book *Against the Heresies* (III:1) he writes as follows:

"Matthew published his Gospel among the Hebrews in their dialect whilst Peter and Paul were preaching the Word and founding the Church at Rome. After their departure Mark, who was the disciple and interpreter of Peter, handed down to us in writing what Peter had taught. Luke, the follower of Paul, put into a book the Gospel preached by his master. Finally, John, the disciple of the Lord, who also reclined upon his breast, published his Gospel while he was living at Ephesus in Asia" (Quoted by Eusebius in his *Ecclesiastical History*, v:8).*

(3) The document known as the *Muratorian Canon* is a fragment of a translation into barbarous Latin, by a careless and ignorant scribe of the eighth century,

* At first sight this passage seems to suggest that Matthew's Gospel was not written until Peter and Paul had both arrived in Rome, and that Mark's Gospel was not written until after Peter's death. In *The Journal of Theological Studies,* July 1905, pp. 563 ff., Dom Chapman showed that Irenaeus had no intention of dating the writing of the Gospels. His interpretation of the passage is as follows:

"Matthew among the Hebrews in their own language published a writing of the Gospel [besides preaching it]. Peter and Paul preaching the Gospel [not to the Jews but] at Rome [without writing it down], and founding the church there [whose testimony I shall give presently, viz. III 3]. But [although they died without having written a Gospel] after their death [their preaching has not been lost to us, for] Mark, the disciple and interpreter of Peter, has handed down to us, he also in writing [like Matthew], the things which were preached by Peter. And Luke besides, the companion of [the other] Paul, set down in a book the Gospel preached by that Apostle. Finally, John, the disciple of the Lord, he also published a Gospel while he was living in Ephesus of Asia."

of a Greek original dating probably from the end of the second century. There can be little doubt that its first words refer to St. Mark's presence at St. Peter's instructions in Rome:

". . . at which he [St. Mark] was present and thus set them down. The third book of the Gospel is according to Luke. Luke, the physician, whom, after the Ascension of Christ, Paul had taken to himself as travelling companion,* wrote in his own name what he had been told, although he had not himself seen the Lord in the flesh. And so, as far as he could learn them, he set down the events beginning with the birth of John [the Baptist]. The fourth book of the Gospels is that of John, one of the disciples. When his fellow-disciples and bishops urged him [to write his Gospel], he said: 'Fast with me for three days from to-day, and then let us relate to each other whatever may be revealed to each one of us.' On that very night it was revealed to Andrew, one of the Apostles, that John should narrate in his own name everything that they all remembered."

(4) Clement of Alexandria, who died about 215, composed a work entitled *Hypotyposes,* which has not come down to us. According to Eusebius this book gave "abridged accounts of all the canonical Scriptures, including even those that are disputed." In the following passage Eusebius quotes verbally from Clement's *Hypotyposes:*

* In the Latin *ut juris studiosum,* usually amended to *ut itineris socium.* The obscurity of this phrase does not affect the document in any serious way.

"In the same work Clement gives the tradition concerning the order of the Gospels, as derived from the oldest presbyters, in this manner: He says that those which contain the genealogies [viz. Matthew and Luke] were written first, but that the Gospel of Mark was occasioned thus: 'When Peter publicly preached the Word of God at Rome, and published the Gospel by the Spirit, those who were present, being numerous, besought Mark, as having followed him for many years and remembering his words, to write down what he said. And when Mark had done so, he gave the Gospel to those who had asked for it. Peter knew of this, and neither forbade nor encouraged it. Last of all, John, perceiving that what had reference to the body [i.e. the bodily life of Christ] was sufficiently handed down, at the request of his familiar friends and inspired by the Holy Ghost, wrote a spiritual Gospel' " (Eusebius, *Ecclesiastical History*, VI:14).

(5) Origen died in 251. He had been a disciple of Clement of Alexandria, and his Commentaries on the Scriptures were famous. The following passage from Eusebius preserves the actual words of Origen:

"In the first book of his *Commentaries on the Gospel of Matthew,* he Origen attests that there are only four Gospels, in these words: 'The tradition I have received respecting the four Gospels which alone are undisputed throughout the Church of God on earth, is as follows: The first is according to Matthew, who was once a publican and afterwards became an Apostle of Jesus Christ. This Gospel was designed for Jewish converts and was written in Hebrew. The second is that according to Mark, which was written as Peter expounded it—Mark being the man he acknowledges as his son in his Catholic Epistle, saying: 'The Church that is in Babylon, elected together with you, saluteth you, and so doth my son Mark.' The third is according to Luke, which is commended by Paul. It was written for the Gentiles. The last is the Gospel of John. . . . What shall we say of John, the man who reclined on the breast of Christ and who has left but one Gospel, although in it he confesses that it would have been possible for him to write more books than the world could contain?' " (*Ecclesiastical History*, VI:25).

(6) Tertullian (c. 220) writes as follows against Marcion, who early in the second century had rejected all the Gospels save that of Luke, and even this he retained only in a garbled version:

"If it is agreed that that is truer which is earlier, and that that is earlier which was from the beginning, and that that was from the beginning which was from the Apostles —then it will also hold good that that was handed down by the Apostles which the Churches of the Apostles have kept as a sacred deposit. . . . I therefore maintain that in these Churches, and not only in the Apostolic Churches but in all the Churches which are united to them by the bond of the Sacrament, that Gospel of Luke has from its very earliest publication stood its ground. . . . And the same authority of the Apostolic Churches will stand guarantee for the other Gospels, too, which we hold through them and according to their usage: I mean the Gospels of John and Matthew. Moreover the Gospel which Mark published may be termed Peter's, for Mark was his interpreter; just as people are wont to assign Luke's digest to

Paul. And indeed what the disciple publishes should rightly be assigned to his master" (*Adversus Marcionem,* IV:4).

(7) Eusebius, Bishop of Caesarea, wrote his *Ecclesiastical History* about 325. In it he not only preserves extensive quotations from ancient authors, but also records his own version of the traditions concerning the Gospels, as follows:

"Of all the disciples of the Lord only Matthew and John have left us written memorials, and they, according to tradition, only wrote from necessity. For Matthew, who had at first preached to the Hebrews, when he was about to go to other peoples committed his Gospel to writing in his native tongue, and thus compensated for the loss of his presence those whom he was obliged to leave. And they say that when Mark and Luke had already published their Gospels, John, who had employed all his time in publishing the Gospel orally, finally proceeded to write, and this for the following reasons: The three Gospels having come into the hands of all and into his own [John's], they say that he accepted them and bore witness to their truthfulness, but that there was lacking in them an account of the deeds done by Christ at the outset of his ministry. And this indeed is true. For it is evident that the three [other] evangelists recorded only the deeds done by the Saviour for one year after the imprisonment of John the Baptist. . . . They say therefore, that the Apostle John, being asked to do it for this reason, gave in his Gospel an account of the period which had been omitted by the earlier evangelists, and of the deeds performed by the Saviour during that period—that is, of those things which were done before the imprisonment of the Baptist" (*Ecclesiastical History*, III:24).

(8) St. Jerome, who died in 420, is acknowledged on all hands as the most learned of Biblical scholars in the early centuries, and as a great authority not only on the text but also on the primitive traditions about the sacred writers. In the Prologue to his *Commentaries on the Gospels of St. Matthew* he writes as follows:

"The first of all the evangelists is Matthew the publican, surnamed Levi, who published his Gospel in Judaea in the Hebrew tongue. He wrote it chiefly for the sake of those Jews who had believed in Jesus and no longer maintained the shadow of the [old] Law which was now at length dissipated by the truth of the Gospel.

"The second is Mark, the interpreter of the Apostle Peter and the first Bishop of the Alexandrian Church, who himself did not see the Lord and Saviour but narrated, faithfully rather than in order, those things which he had heard his master preach.

"The third is Luke the physician, a Syrian of Antioch by birth, 'whose praise is in the Gospel,' a disciple of the Apostle Paul. He wrote his volume in the districts of Achaia and Boeotia. Some things he derived from older sources, and, as he himself acknowledges in his Prologue, he described what he had heard about rather than what he had actually seen.

"The last is John, the Apostle and Evangelist, whom Jesus loved exceedingly and who, reclining on the Lord's breast, drank therefrom the purest streams of doctrine."

Further information about each of the evangelists is provided in St. Jerome's *Catalogue of Ecclesiastical Writers:*

"Matthew, who is also called Levi, and who from a publican became an Apostle, was the first to put together in Judaea, for the sake of those of the circumcision who had believed, the Gospel of Christ. He did this in Hebrew characters and words. But who afterwards translated it into Greek is by no means clear. As a matter of fact the Hebrew text is still preserved in the library at Caesarea which Pamphilus the martyr so laboriously collected. And I myself had an opportunity of copying it afforded me by the Nazarenes of Beroea in Syria who use this text (*volumine*). I would only remark here that wherever the evangelist, whether in his own person or in that of Our Lord and Saviour, appears to misquote the Old Testament, he is not following the authority of the Septuagint translation but the Hebrew: for example when he writes 'Out of Egypt have I called my Son' and 'that he shall be called a Nazarite' " (III).

"Mark, the disciple and interpreter of Peter, wrote at the petition of the brethren in Rome a brief Gospel according to what he had heard Peter preaching. And when Peter heard of this he approved it and of his own authority ordered it to be read in the Churches, as Clement in the Sixth Book of his *Outlines* and Papias the Bishop of Hierapolis tell us. And Peter mentions this same Mark in his first Epistle where he speaks of Rome under the figure of Babylon: 'The Church that is in Babylon, elected together with you, saluteth you, and so doth my son Mark.' Taking with him his Gospel, Mark passed into Egypt. He was the first to preach Christ at Alexandria where he founded the Church. . . . Mark died in the eighth year of Nero and was buried at Alexandria" (VIII).

"Luke, a physician of Antioch, knew well the Greek language as his writings show. He was one of St. Paul's train, and, as the companion of all his journeyings, he wrote his Gospel. Of him Paul says: 'We have sent also with him the brother whose praise is in the Gospel through all the Churches'; and to the Colossians he says: 'Luke, the most dear physician, saluteth you'; and to Timothy: 'Luke alone is with me.' Luke also published another notable volume which bears the title 'Acts of Apostles'; in this volume the history is carried down to the two years of St. Paul's sojourn at Rome, that is to the fourth year of Nero. This shows us that the book was composed at Rome. . . . Some think that whenever St. Paul in his Epistles says 'according to my Gospel,' he is referring to Luke's volume; also that Luke not only learnt his Gospel from the Apostle Paul who had not known the Lord in the flesh, but from the other Apostles as well. Indeed Luke himself states this in the beginning of his book when he says: 'According as they have delivered them unto us who from the beginning were eye-witnesses and ministers of the Word.' The Gospel Luke wrote according to what he had heard [from others]; but the Acts he composed according to what he himself had seen. Luke lies buried at Constantinople whither his bones, together with the relics of the Apostle Andrew, were translated in the twentieth year of Constantine" (VII).

"The Apostle John, whom Jesus loved exceedingly, was the son of Zebedee and the brother of the Apostle James whom Herod put to death after the Lord's Passion. He wrote his Gospel last of all and, at the request of the bishops of Asia, as an antidote to Cerinthus and other heretics, and particularly against the then current teaching of the Ebionites who asserted that Christ did not exist previous to Mary. Consequently John was compelled to declare his divine Birth. Other reasons, too, are given for his writing: namely that, having read the Gospels of Matthew, Mark and Luke, he approved of the history as they had set it forth and declared that they had told the truth. But John perceived that they had only told the history of one year, that, namely, in which Christ suffered after John's imprisonment. Omitting, then, the year the events of which had been chronicled by the three previous evangelists, John told the story of the time which preceded the Baptist's imprisonment, and this will be patent to anyone who reads the four Gospels carefully. This fact serves to explain the apparent want of agreement between John and the other three" (IX).

(9) St. Augustine, Bishop of Hippo (died 430), discusses the order of the four Gospels in the following passage:

"First Matthew, then Mark, then Luke, lastly John. As far, then, as their respective knowledge of and preaching of the Gospels is concerned, their mutual order is not the same as the order in which they wrote the Gospel. For as far as knowledge and preaching are concerned, those were the first who followed the Lord when present in the flesh, who heard him speaking and witnessed his deeds, and who by his command were sent to preach the Gospel. But in writing the Gospel—a task which was, we must suppose, divinely committed to them—two of the number of those whom the Lord chose before his Passion occupy the first and last place respectively, Matthew the first, John the last. While the two who remain were not of their number, yet none the less did they follow the Christ who spoke within them. . . . Of these four Matthew alone wrote in Hebrew, the others in Greek. And while each of them would seem to have retained his own method of writing, yet no one of them seems to have written in ignorance of what his predecessor had written, nor to have omitted in ignorance what another had given, but, according as each one was inspired, he added to the whole the cooperation of a toil which was not superfluous. For Matthew undertook to speak of the Lord's Incarnation according to his kingly ancestry as well as of many of his sayings and doings according to man's present life. Mark followed Matthew almost as a servant would follow his master, and gave a shortened version of his book. Mark has nothing in common with John alone; very little of his Gospel is peculiar to him; he has a few things in common with Luke alone; but he has very many things which are also in Matthew; indeed he narrates many things in precisely the same words as Matthew does, either alone or agreeing with the other Gospels. Luke seems to be more concerned with the priestly character and origin of the Lord" (*De Consensu Evangeliorum*, 1:2).

II. DECISIONS OF THE BIBLICAL COMMISSION

(1) *Concerning the Authorship, Date of Composition, and Historical Truth of the Gospel according to Matthew* (19 June 1911)

To the following questions which have been proposed, the Pontifical Biblical Commission has decided to reply in this manner:

(i) On the basis of the universal and constant agreement of the Church from the earliest centuries, which is clearly supported by the witness of the Fathers, the titles of the Gospel manuscripts, the oldest versions of the Sacred Books and the catalogues drawn up by the holy Fathers, by the ecclesiastical writers, by the Supreme Pontiffs and the Councils, and finally by the liturgical use of the Church both in the East and in the West—can it be, and must it be, affirmed for certain that Matthew, the Apostle of Christ, is really the author of the Gospel which is known by his name?

Reply: In the Affirmative.

(ii) Can it be held that there is sufficient basis in tradition for the opinion that Matthew wrote before the other Evangelists? also that he wrote this first Gospel in the native tongue then used by the Jews of Palestine to whom he addressed his work?

Reply: In the Affirmative to both points.

(iii) Can the publication of this original text be referred to a time subsequent to the destruction of Jerusalem, so that the prophecies it contains concerning that same destruction would have been written after the event?

Moreover is the oft-quoted testimony of Irenaeus (*Adversus Haereses,* III:1) *—the interpretation of

* See above, p. 66.

which is uncertain and a matter of controversy—to be considered sufficiently weighty to compel us to reject the opinion that it is more in accordance with tradition to say that publication of Matthew's original text preceded the arrival of St. Paul in Rome?

Reply: In the Negative on both points.

(iv) Can that opinion of some modern writers be upheld as at all probable, which maintains that Matthew did not properly and strictly compose the Gospel as it has come down to us, but merely made a collection of the sayings or discourses of Christ, and that some other anonymous author—whom they term the redactor of the Gospel—made use of this collection as his source?

Reply: In the Negative.

(v) In view of the fact that the Fathers and all ecclesiastical writers, and the Church herself from her very beginnings, use as canonical only the Greek text of the Gospel known as Matthew's—not even excepting those who expressly declare that the Apostle Matthew wrote in his native tongue—can it be proved for certain that this Greek Gospel is substantially identical with that which the same author wrote in his native tongue?

Reply: In the Affirmative.

(vi) In view of the fact that the author of the first Gospel has an especially dogmatic and apologetic purpose—namely to prove to the Jews that Jesus is the Messias foretold by the Prophets and born of the stock of David—and that, moreover, in arranging the deeds and discourses which he narrates and records he does not always follow the chronological order; is it allowable to argue that these things are not to be accepted as true?

And can it further be affirmed that the accounts of Christ's deeds and sayings which are in this Gospel have undergone a certain alteration and adaptation under the influence of the Old Testament prophecies and of the more mature state at which the Church had arrived, and that in consequence they hardly correspond with historical truth?

Reply: In the Negative on both points.

(vii) Ought we to single out as especially destitute of solid foundation the views of those who call in question the historical authenticity of the first two chapters in which the genealogy and infancy of Christ are narrated, as also the authenticity of certain pronouncements which are of great dogmatic importance, such as those referring to the Primacy of Peter (xvi 17-19), the formula for Baptism and the world-wide commission given to the Apostles of preaching the Gospel (xxviii 19-20), and other things of this kind, which are recounted in a special way in St. Matthew?

Reply: In the Affirmative.

(2) *Concerning the Authorship, Date of Composition, and Historical Truth of the Gospels according to Mark and according to Luke* (26 June 1912)

To the following questions which have been proposed, the Pontifical Biblical Commission has decided to reply in this manner:

(i) Does the clear voice of tradition—which from the beginning of the Church is so remarkably unanimous and is confirmed by so many proofs, namely by the express testimonies of the holy Fathers and the ecclesiastical writers, by quotations and allusions which occur in their writings, by the use made of them by the ancient heretics, by the versions of the books of the New Testament, by the oldest manuscripts which are to be found almost everywhere, and also by the internal evidence of the text of the Sacred Books themselves—does this clear voice of tradition compel us to affirm as certain that Mark, the disciple and interpreter of Peter, and Luke the physician, the helper and companion of Paul, were really the authors of the Gospels which are attributed to them?

Reply: In the Affirmative.

(ii) Are the reasons whereby some critics strive to prove that the last twelve verses of Mark's Gospel (xvi 9-20) were not written by Mark himself but added by another hand—are these reasons of such force as to justify us in affirming that the verses in question are not to be received as inspired and canonical? At any rate do they prove that Mark is not the author of these verses?

Reply: In the Negative to both questions.

(iii) Similarly is it lawful to question the inspiration and canonicity of Luke's narratives of the Infancy of Christ (i 2) or of the appearance of the Angel strengthening Jesus and of the Sweat of Blood (xxii 43 f.)? And can it be shown by solid reasons—as ancient heretics were pleased to do, and as some modern critics would like to think—that these narratives do not belong to the genuine Gospel of Luke?

Reply: In the Negative to both questions.

(iv) With regard to those very rare and altogether singular documents in which the canticle *Magnificat* is attributed to Elizabeth and not to the Blessed Virgin Mary, can they and ought they to weigh against the unanimous witness of almost all the manuscripts both of the original Greek text and of the translations, as well as against the interpretation plainly demanded both by the context and by the mental attitude of Our Lady herself and also by the constant tradition of the Church?

Reply: In the Negative.

(v) With regard to the chronological order of the Gospels, is it lawful to abandon the view which, being founded upon the most ancient and constant witness of tradition, maintains that after Matthew (who first of them all wrote his Gospel in his native tongue) Mark wrote second in order and Luke third?

And must we regard as contrary to this view the opinion which asserts that the second and third Gospels were composed before the Greek version of the first Gospel?

Reply: In the Negative to both questions.

(vi) Is it lawful to defer the date of the composition of Mark's and Luke's Gospels until after the destruction of Jerusalem?

Or can it be held that—because in Luke Our Lord's prophecy of the destruction of this city seems to be more definite—this Gospel was written after the siege had begun?

Reply: In the Negative to both questions.

(vii) Ought we to affirm that Luke's Gospel preceded the book of the Acts of the Apostles which he also wrote (Acts i 1 ff.)? and that since this later book was finished towards the end of St. Paul's imprisonment at Rome, Luke's Gospel was not written after that date?

Reply: In the Affirmative.

(viii) Bearing in mind not only the evidence of tradition but also the internal proofs with regard to the sources which the Evangelists used in writing their Gospels, can we prudently call in question the view that Mark wrote according to the preaching of Peter, and Luke according to the preaching of Paul, and that these Evangelists had other trustworthy sources, either oral or written?

Reply: In the Negative.

(ix) Can the words and deeds which Mark narrates

accurately and even graphically according to Peter's preaching, and which Luke expounds most carefully "having diligently attained to all things from the beginning" by manifestly trustworthy witnesses "who from the beginning were eye-witnesses and ministers of the Word" (Luke i 2 ff.)—can these words and deeds claim that full historical trust which the Church has always accorded them?

Or, on the contrary, are these same words and deeds to be considered as devoid, at least in part, of historical truth, either because the writers were not eye-witnesses, or because in each Gospel we may frequently detect defects of order and discrepancies in the succession of events, or because, since the writers came and wrote later, they necessarily relate ideas alien to the mind of Christ and of the Apostles or deeds more or less distorted by the popular imagination, or finally because each writer has indulged, according to his scope, in preconceived dogmatic notions?

Reply: In the Affirmative to the first question; in the Negative to the second.

(3) *Concerning the Synoptic Problem and the Mutual Relationship between the First Three Gospels* (26 June 1912)

To the following questions which have been proposed, the Pontifical Biblical Commission has decided to reply in this manner:

(i) Provided that they maintain those things which according to the above decisions must be maintained—

especially with regard to the authenticity and integrity of the three Gospels of Matthew, Mark and Luke, with regard to the substantial identity of the Greek Gospel of Matthew with its primitive original, and with regard to the chronological order in which these Gospels were written—is it lawful for exegetes who seek to explain the similarities and dissimilarities of these Gospels, to dispute freely among the many varied and contradictory opinions of writers, and to appeal to hypotheses as regards the way in which the Gospels were handed down whether orally or in writing or by the dependence of one Gospel upon its predecessor or predecessors?

Reply: In the Affirmative.

(ii) Ought they to be considered as upholding the foregoing decrees who, without the support of any testimony of tradition or historical proof, readily embrace the hypothesis commonly known as the Two-Document hypothesis, whereby they seek to explain the composition of the Greek Gospel of Matthew and of the Gospel of Luke mainly by their dependence upon the Gospel of Mark and upon a so-called collection of the Words of the Lord?

And, moreover, may they freely defend this hypothesis?

Reply: In the Negative to both questions.

(4) *Concerning the Authorship and the Historical Truth of the Fourth Gospel* (29 May 1907)

To the following questions which have been proposed, the Pontifical Biblical Commission has replied thus:

(i) In view of the constant, universal and solemn tradition of the Church from the second century—a tradition which is especially evident in these four ways: (a) From the testimonies and allusions of the holy Fathers, of ecclesiastical writers and of heretics, which, being necessarily derived from the disciples of the Apostles or their first successors, must be connected with the origin of the book; (b) from the accepted authorship of the fourth Gospel in the canon and lists of the Sacred Books; (c) from the oldest manuscripts of the same Books and from the translations into various languages; and (d) from the public liturgical use obtaining everywhere from the very beginning of the Church—apart from any theological argument, is the historical argument that the Apostle John is the author of the fourth Gospel sufficiently strong as not to be weakened in any way by the reasons which the critics have adduced against this tradition?

Reply: In the Affirmative.

(ii) Moreover, with regard to the internal arguments which are based on the actual text of the fourth Gospel and on the evidence of the writer and the clear relationship between his Gospel and the first Epistle of John the Apostle—are these same internal arguments to be considered as confirming the tradition which unhesitatingly attributes the fourth Gospel to the same Apostle?

Further, can the difficulties resulting from the collation of this Gospel with the other three be reasonably solved—as indeed the holy Fathers and Catholic exegetes have always striven to solve them—in the light of the differences of time, of scope and of the readers for whom and against whom the author wrote?

Reply: In the Affirmative to both questions.

(iii) Notwithstanding the practice, which has flourished in the universal Church from the earliest times, of arguing from the fourth Gospel as from a strictly historical document, and on the other hand taking into consideration the peculiar character of this Gospel and the author's clear intention of showing and proving the divinity of Christ from the very deeds and words of Our Lord—can it be said that the events narrated in the fourth Gospel were entirely or partly made up to serve as allegories or doctrinal symbols, and that the discourses of Our Lord were not really spoken by him but are the theological compositions of the author although he put them into Our Lord's mouth?

Reply: In the Negative.